FACT FILE
DINOSAURS

p

This is a Parragon book
First published in 2006

Parragon
Queen Street House
4 Queen Street
Bath BA1 1HE, UK

Copyright © Parragon Books Ltd 2006

ISBN 1-40548-062-9
Printed in China

Contents

What is a Dinosaur?

Millions of years ago, Earth was home to many types of prehistoric creatures. One of these groups of creatures we now know as dinosaurs. The name 'dinosaur' means 'terrible lizard'.

For a prehistoric creature to be classed as a dinosaur, it has to have the following characteristics:
- dinosaurs lived between 220 and 65 million years ago;
- they lived on land; • they could not fly;
- they had straight legs tucked underneath their bodies;
- they were reptiles.

When did Dinosaurs Live?

The Triassic Period

The first dinosaur fossils occur in rocks dating back to the Middle Triassic period, about 220 million years ago. The world was very different then. The climate was warmer and less moist. Vast areas of land were dry scrub and desert, with tough, shrubby plants, and fewer trees than today.

The central regions of the vast Triassic supercontinent were far from the sea. Great deserts developed, where the thin soil was blown over bare, rocky uplands.

The Triassic world did not have climate zones as we know them today. There was no ice at the poles. In fact, the single vast continent of Pangaea drifted towards the North Pole, while the South Pole was open ocean. Temperatures varied from mild to hot; rain was sparse.

In the valleys, small rivers flowed during the rainy season. But their beds were dry much of the year.

The Jurassic Period

As the Triassic gave way to the Jurassic, around 200 million years ago, climates began to change. Global temperatures started to cool, although it was still warm by today's standards. Rainfall increased, bringing damp lushness to many regions that were previously parched. Dinosaurs grew to their greatest size.

The break-up of the continents began, meaning that more regions were nearer the sea, where moist winds could bring rain to the land. With this extra rainfall, and less extreme heat, forests spread from valleys to cloak large areas of uplands.

In lowland areas, huge swamps and bogs formed, similar to the 'coal forests' of the Carboniferous period, 150 million years previously. The climate was much the same all over the world. The long, mild rainy seasons were only rarely broken, as short, dry periods shrank the rivers and lakes slightly.

Plentiful rivers and lakes encouraged fish, which some dinosaurs relied on for food.

The Cretaceous Period

The Cretaceous, at 80 million years, was the longest period of the Mesozoic Era. It saw the beginning of the climate zones we have today, being colder near the Poles and warmer towards the Equator, where tropical forests began to form.

The Cretaceous was one of the most active times of mountain-building on Earth. Lava and fumes poured from volcanoes. Drifting continents threw up massive rumples and wrinkles in the planet's outer rocky layer, the crust.

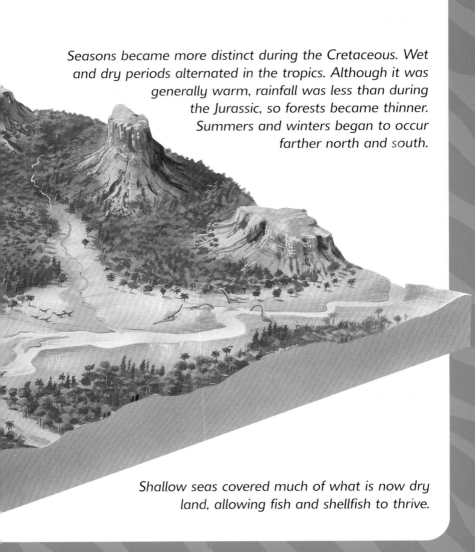

Seasons became more distinct during the Cretaceous. Wet and dry periods alternated in the tropics. Although it was generally warm, rainfall was less than during the Jurassic, so forests became thinner. Summers and winters began to occur farther north and south.

Shallow seas covered much of what is now dry land, allowing fish and shellfish to thrive.

Giant Plant-eating Dinosaurs

Sauropods were a group of plant-eating dinosaurs (herbivores). Their name means 'lizard feet'. The first sauropods appeared about 200 million years ago. Plant-eating dinosaurs were mainly found during the Jurassic period. The last of the sauropods died about 65 million years ago.

Features

Sauropods walked on all-fours, on thick, pillar-like legs. They had long necks which helped them reach the tops of trees to eat the foliage. Sauropods were large and powerful which helped them to defend themselves. Their feet and tails could cause serious injury to other dinosaurs.

Meat-eating Dinosaurs

Meat-eating dinosaurs (carnivores) are a group of dinosaurs called theropods. Their name means 'beast feet'. The first theropods appeared about 220 million years ago. Meat-eating dinosaurs survived for 160 million years, right until the time that dinosaurs died out, 65 million years ago.

Features

Most meat-eating dinosaurs walked on two slender legs that ended in three-toed, bird-like feet with sharp claws. They were able to move quite fast. They had either teeth or beaks. Theropod teeth were thin and blade-like, with serrated ridges that hooked into their victim's flesh. Toothless theropods had bony beaks to crack open eggs.

Plated, Armoured, Horned and Bone-headed Dinosaurs

Plated Dinosaurs
These were the stegosaurs – medium- to large-sized plant-eaters that walked on all-fours and which had several upright plates and spines growing from their backs and along their tails.

Armoured Dinosaurs
These were the nodosaurs and the ankylosaurs – medium-sized herbivores that walked on four short legs. Their bodies had bony plates embedded in the skin. Some had short body spines, others had tail clubs.

Horned and Bone-headed Dinosaurs
Horned dinosaurs were called ceratopsians and bone-headed dinosaurs were named pachycephalosaurs. Some walked on all-fours while others walked on two legs. All of these types of dinosaur were plant-eaters.

Duck-bills and Other Dinosaurs

Heterodontosaurs
Heterodontosaurs were a family of dinosaurs characterized by their different kinds of teeth – used for cutting, chewing or stabbing. They appeared in the early Jurassic period and were the first of the ornithopods.

Hypsilophodonts
Hypsilophodonts were characterized by high-ridged, chisel-shaped cheek teeth.

Iguanodonts
Iguanodonts had many small, ridged cheek teeth which were tightly packed together.

Hadrosaurs
Hadrosaurs – meaning 'big lizards' – are often called by their nickname 'duck-bills' because of the duck-like shape of their beaks.

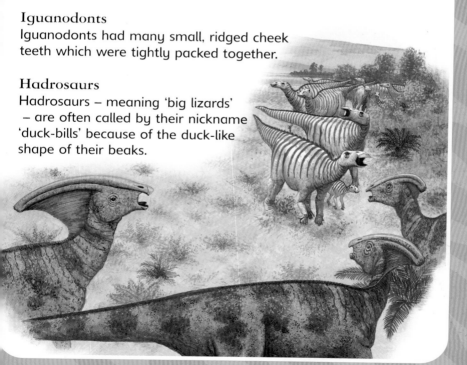

DINOSAUR FACT FILE

Tyrannosaurus Rex

(say *tie-ran-oh-sore-us*)

• I am a	bipedal carnivore
• My family was	Tyrannosaurs
• My name means	'Tyrant lizard'
• I lived in the	Late Cretaceous period, about 70 million years ago
• My home was	North America; Asia
• My length was	12 metres (40 feet) long
• My weight was	8 tonnes (approx. 8 tons)

It had huge teeth with saw-like edges for biting, gripping and ripping prey.

Ankylosaurus

(say *an-kee-loh-sore-us*)

• I am a	quadrupedal herbivore
• My family was	Ankylosaurs
• My name means	'Stiff lizard'
• I lived in the	Late Cretaceous period, about 70 million years ago
• My home was	North America
• My length was	10 metres (33 feet)
• My weight was	5 tonnes (approx. 5 tons)

Two rows of spikes grew along its back, and horns poked from the back of its head.

Its wide beak and small teeth were perfect for nipping off low-growing plants.

Its tail ended in a wide, bony club.

Oviraptor

(say *oh-vee-rap-tor*)

• I am a	bipedal carnivore
• My family was	Oviraptors
• My name means	'Egg thief'
• I lived in the	Late Cretaceous period, about 80 million years ago
• My home was	Asia (what is now Mongolia)
• My length was	1.8 metres (6 feet)
• My weight was	20 kilograms (44 pounds)

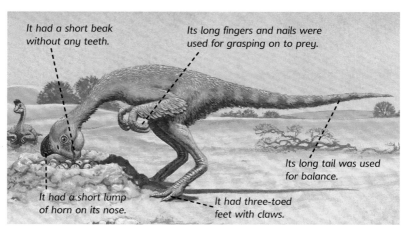

It had a short beak without any teeth.

Its long fingers and nails were used for grasping on to prey.

Its long tail was used for balance.

It had a short lump of horn on its nose.

It had three-toed feet with claws.

Baryonyx
(say *bar-ee-on-icks*)

• I am a	bipedal carnivore
• My family was	Baryonychids
• My name means	'Heavy claw'
• I lived in the	Early Cretaceous period, about 120 million years ago
• My home was	England
• My length was	10 metres (33 feet)
• My weight was	2 tonnes (approx. 2 tons)

It had a long, stiff tail.

Baryonyx had a long, straight neck.

Its arms were powerful.

It had a long, low snout

Iguanodon
(say *ig-wha-no-don*)

• I am a	bipedal/quadrupedal herbivore
• My family was	Iguanodonts
• My name means	'Iguana tooth'
• I lived in the	Early Cretaceous period, about 130 million years ago
• My home was	Europe; North America
• My length was	10 metres (33 feet)
• My weight was	5 tonnes (approx. 5 tons)

Its snout ended in a blunt, toothless beak.

Its long tail was stiffened by bony tendons.

Iguanodon had three-toed hind feet with hooves.

Maiasaura

(say *may-ah-sore-ah*)

• I am a	bipedal/quadrupedal herbivore
• My family was	Hadrosaurs
• My name means	'Good mother lizard'
• I lived in the	Late Cretaceous period, about 80 million years ago
• My home was	North America
• My length was	9 metres (30 feet)
• My weight was	3 tonnes (approx. 3 tons)

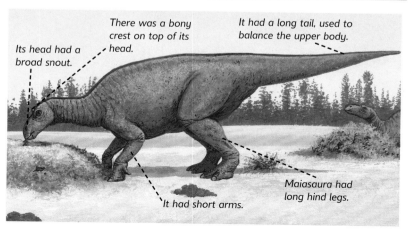

There was a bony crest on top of its head.

It had a long tail, used to balance the upper body.

Its head had a broad snout.

It had short arms.

Maiasaura had long hind legs.

Diplodocus
(say *die-ploh-do-kus*)

• I am a	quadrupedal herbivore
• My family was	Sauropods
• My name means	'Double-beam lizard'
• I lived in the	Late Jurassic period, about 150 million years ago
• My home was	North America
• My length was	27 metres (88 feet)
• My weight was	12 tonnes (approx. 12 tons)

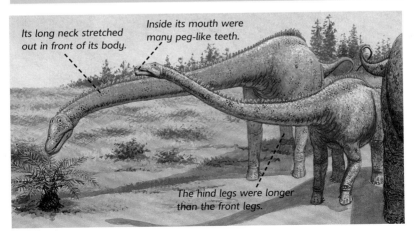

Its long neck stretched out in front of its body.

Inside its mouth were many peg-like teeth.

The hind legs were longer than the front legs.

Titanosaurus

(say *tie-tan-oh-sore-us*)

• I am a	quadrupel herbivore
• My family was	Sauropods
• My name means	'Titanic lizard'
• I lived in the	Late Cretaceous period, about 70 million years ago
• My home was	Asia
• My length was	20 metres (66 feet)
• My weight was	18 tonnes (approx. 18 tons)

It had a small head and long neck.

It had a big, heavy body.

It walked on four, thick pillar-like legs.

Stegoceras

(say *ste-goss-er-as*)

• I am a	bipedal herbivore
• My family was	Pachycephalosaurs
• My name means	'Horny roof'
• I lived in the	Late Cretaceous period, about 70 million years ago
• My home was	North America
• My length was	2 metres (6 feet)
• My weight was	55 kilograms (121 pounds)

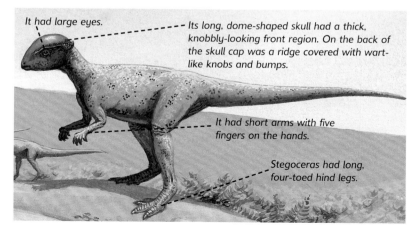

It had large eyes.

Its long, dome-shaped skull had a thick, knobbly-looking front region. On the back of the skull cap was a ridge covered with wart-like knobs and bumps.

It had short arms with five fingers on the hands.

Stegoceras had long, four-toed hind legs.

Deinonychus

(say *die-non-ick-us*)

- **I am a**   bipedal carnivore
- **My family was**   Raptors
- **My name means**   'Terrible claw'
- **I lived in the**   Early Cretaceous period, about 110 million years ago
- **My home was**   North America
- **My length was**   3 metres (10 feet)
- **My weight was**   80 kilograms (176 pounds)

It had the large eyes of a hunter, suggesting that its eyesight was good.

The slender neck was curved and flexible.

On the second toe of the foot was a long, curved claw – a deadly weapon.

Its arms were long and its three-fingered hands were very large with powerful, sharply curved talons.

Lesothosaurus

(say *le-soo-too-sore-us*)

• I am a	bipedal herbivore
• My family was	Ornithopods
• My name means	'Lizard from Lesotho'
• I lived in the	Early Jurassic period, about 200 million years ago
• My home was	Africa
• My length was	1 metre (3 feet)
• My weight was	30 kilograms (66 pounds)

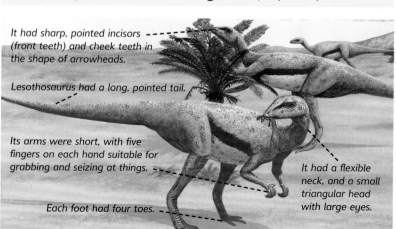

It had sharp, pointed incisors (front teeth) and cheek teeth in the shape of arrowheads.

Lesothosaurus had a long, pointed tail.

Its arms were short, with five fingers on each hand suitable for grabbing and seizing at things.

Each foot had four toes.

It had a flexible neck, and a small triangular head with large eyes.

Triceratops

(say *try-ser-a-tops*)

• I am a	quadrupedal herbivore
• My family was	Ceratopsids
• My name means	'Three-horned face'
• I lived in the	Late Cretaceous period, about 70 million years ago
• My home was	North America
• My length was	9 metres (30 feet)
• My weight was	5 tonnes (approx. 5 tons)

It had long brow horns made of solid bone that could be used as defensive weapons.

A solid bone neck frill grew out of the rear skull bones.

Stegosaurus
(say *ste-go-sore-us*)

• I am a	quadrupedal herbivore
• My family was	Stegosaurs
• My name means	'Roofed lizard'
• I lived in the	Late Jurassic period, about 150 million years ago
• My home was	North America
• My length was	up to 9 metres (30 feet)
• My weight was	2 tonnes (approx. 2 tons)

Its bony plates may have been flat, arranged in pairs or on alternating sides.

It had a horned tail for defence against predators.

Its small head contained a tiny brain.

Brachiosaurus

(say *brak-ee-oh-sore-us*)

• I am a	quadrupedal herbivore
• My family was	Sauropods
• My name means	'Arm lizard'
• I lived in the	Late Jurassic period, about 150 million years ago
• My home was	North America; Africa
• My length was	25 metres (82 feet)
• My weight was	30–50 tonnes (approx. 30–50 tons)

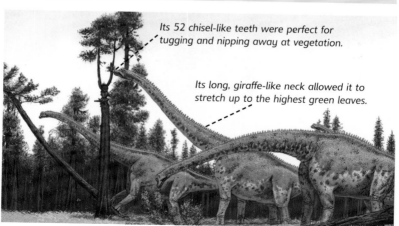

Its 52 chisel-like teeth were perfect for tugging and nipping away at vegetation.

Its long, giraffe-like neck allowed it to stretch up to the highest green leaves.

Giganotosaurus

(say *jy-ga-no-toe-sore-us*)

• I am a	bipedal carnivore
• My family was	Carnosaurs
• My name means	'Giant southern lizard'
• I lived in the	Late Cretaceous period, about 100 million years ago
• My home was	South America
• My length was	16 metres (52 feet)
• My weight was	8 tonnes (approx. 8 tons)

Its eyes stared straight ahead, like those of an eagle.

Inside its large, powerful jaws were many narrow teeth, pointed like arrowheads and serrated along their edges.

It had short arms with three fingers on each hand.

Giganotosaurus had a huge skull, 1.8 metres (6 feet) long, with a small banana-shaped brain.

Allosaurus

(say *al-oh-sore-us*)

• I am a	bipedal carnivore
• My family was	Carnosaurs
• My name means	'Different lizard'
• I lived in the	Early Cretaceous period, about 140 million years ago
• My home was	North America
• My length was	12 metres (39 feet)
• My weight was	2–5 tonnes (approx. 2–5 tons)

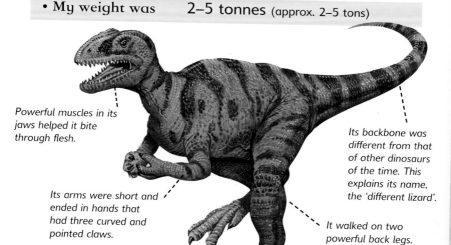

Powerful muscles in its jaws helped it bite through flesh.

Its arms were short and ended in hands that had three curved and pointed claws.

Its backbone was different from that of other dinosaurs of the time. This explains its name, the 'different lizard'.

It walked on two powerful back legs.

33

Janenschia

(say *yah-nen-shee-a*)

• I am a	quadrupedal herbivore
• My family was	Sauropods
• My name means	'Belonging to Janensch'
• I lived in the	Late Jurassic period, about 155 million years ago
• My home was	Africa
• My length was	24 metres (79 feet)
• My weight was	30 tonnes (approx. 30 tons)

Janenschia had a long, flexible neck.

Armoured plates (called scutes) may have been embedded in the leathery skin of its back.

Its long tail was thick and muscular.

It had stumpy, pillar-like legs. The hind legs had long claws on the toes.

Apatosaurus

(say *ah-pat-oh-sore-us*)

• I am a	quadrupedal herbivore
• My family was	Sauropods
• My name means	'Deceptive lizard'
• I lived in the	Late Jurassic period, about 150 million years ago
• My home was	North America
• My length was	21 metres (69 feet)
• My weight was	30 tonnes (approx. 30 tons)

Its nostrils were on top of its head.

For such a massive animal it had a surprisingly small head, which contained a tiny brain and peg-shaped teeth.

Its great weight was carried along on its four tower-like legs. Its hind legs were longer than its front legs.

Its long tail may have been used to fend off attackers.

Each foot had short, stubby toes. Its front feet toes were blunt, but the toes of the back feet ended in claws.

Euoplocephalus
(say *yoo-op-loh-sef-ah-lus*)

• I am a	quadrupedal herbivore
• My family was	Ankylosaurs
• My name means	'Well-armoured head'
• I lived in the	Late Cretaceous period, about 70 million years ago
• My home was	North America
• My length was	6 metres (20 feet)
• My weight was	2 tonnes (approx. 2 tons)

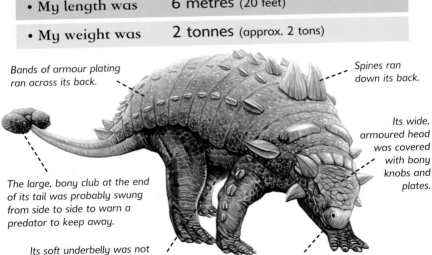

Bands of armour plating ran across its back.

Spines ran down its back.

Its wide, armoured head was covered with bony knobs and plates.

The large, bony club at the end of its tail was probably swung from side to side to warn a predator to keep away.

Its soft underbelly was not armoured. This was its weak spot.

It had a horny, toothless beak. Inside its cheeks were many small, ridged teeth.

Hypsilophodon

(say *hip-sih-loh-foh-don*)

• I am a	bipedal herbivore
• My family was	Hypsilophodonts
• My name means	'High ridge tooth'
• I lived in the	Early Cretaceous period, about 120 million years ago
• My home was	Europe; North America
• My length was	2.3 metres (8 feet)
• My weight was	70 kilograms (154 pounds)

It had a small skull with a horny beak, cheek pouches and large eyes.

Two rows of bony studs may have run down its back.

Its tail, stiffened by bony tendons, was held straight out behind it to balance the front of its body.

It had short arms with five-fingered hands. Each finger was tipped with a sharp claw.

Hypsilophodon had long, slender hind legs for speed and agility. Each foot had four long toes.

Struthiomimus

(say *strooth-ee-oh-mime-us*)

• I am a	bipedal omnivore
• My family was	Ornithomimids
• My name means	'Ostrich mimic'
• I lived in the	Late Cretaceous period, about 70 million years ago
• My home was	North America
• My length was	3.5 metres (11 feet 6 inches)
• My weight was	150 kilograms (330 pounds)

Its neck was long and curved, ending in a small head with a toothless, bird-like beak.

When it ran, it held its tail straight behind it, level with its back.

It had long legs for sprinting.

Kentrosaurus

(say *ken-troh-sore-us*)

• I am a	quadrupedal herbivore
• My family was	Stegosaurs
• My name means	'Spiked lizard'
• I lived in the	Late Jurassic period, about 155 million years ago
• My home was	Africa
• My length was	5 metres (16 feet)
• My weight was	1 tonne (approx. 1 ton)

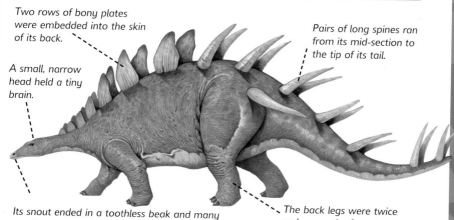

Two rows of bony plates were embedded into the skin of its back.

Pairs of long spines ran from its mid-section to the tip of its tail.

A small, narrow head held a tiny brain.

Its snout ended in a toothless beak and many small teeth were packed inside its cheeks.

The back legs were twice as long as the front legs.

Ornithomimus

(say *or-ni-tho-mee-mus*)

• I am a	bipedal omnivore
• My family was	Ornithomimids
• My name means	'Bird mimic'
• I lived in the	Late Cretaceous period, about 70 million years ago
• My home was	North America
• My length was	3.5 metres (11 feet)
• My weight was	150 kilograms (331 pounds)

Its small head had large eyes and a big brain.

It had a long tail which it held out straight behind it for balance as it ran.

It had a long, toothless horny beak.

Ornithomimus had a short and compact body.

Its short arms ended in hands with three spindly fingers tipped with pointed claws.

It had long, slim legs, each with three clawed toes.

Spinosaurus

(say *spy-no-sore-us*)

• I am a	bipedal carnivore
• My family was	Carnosaurs
• My name means	'Thorn lizard'
• I lived in the	Late Cretaceous period, about 70 million years ago
• My home was	Africa
• My length was	12 metres (40 feet)
• My weight was	7 tonnes (approx. 7 tons)

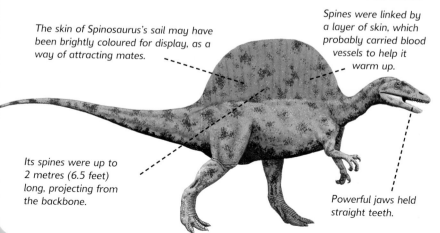

The skin of Spinosaurus's sail may have been brightly coloured for display, as a way of attracting mates.

Spines were linked by a layer of skin, which probably carried blood vessels to help it warm up.

Its spines were up to 2 metres (6.5 feet) long, projecting from the backbone.

Powerful jaws held straight teeth.

Supersaurus

(say *soo-per-sore-us*)

• I am a	quadrupedal herbivore
• My family was	Sauropods
• My name means	'Super lizard'
• I lived in the	Jurassic period, about 150 million years ago
• My home was	North America
• My length was	42 metres (138 feet)
• My weight was	55 tonnes (approx. 55 tons)

Its long tail counterbalanced its long neck.

Its big gut allowed it to digest large amounts of plant material.

Supersaurus had a tiny head and brain.

It had four elephant-like, powerful legs.

It had a long neck for browsing.

Compsognathus

(say *komp-so-nay-thus*)

• **I am a**	bipedal carnivore
• **My family was**	Theropods
• **My name means**	'Elegant jaw'
• **I lived in the**	Late Jurassic period, about 145 million years ago
• **My home was**	Europe
• **My length was**	1 metre (3 feet)
• **My weight was**	3 kilograms (6.5 pounds)

It had a large skull with small, sharp, curved teeth. Its teeth were spaced apart from each other.

Its long, flexible tail took up more than half its length and helped it to keep its balance.

It had short arms which may have had two clawed fingers on each hand.

It had powerful hind legs.

Styracosaurus

(say *sty-rack-oh-sore-us*)

• I am a	quadrupedal herbivore
• My family was	Ceratopsids
• My name means	'Spiked lizard'
• I lived in the	Late Cretaceous period, about 70 million years ago
• My home was	North America
• My length was	5.2 metres (17 feet)
• My weight was	2.7 tonnes (approx. 2.7 tons)

Six long spikes added further protection. They also made the dinosaur look bigger.

A short neck frill protected its neck.

Styracosaurus had a long, straight nose horn.

Its tough hide protected it against the spiky undergrowth.

It used its beaked mouth for cropping a variety of foods.

It had hoofed feet and powerful leg muscles.

Psittacosaurus

(say *sit-ak-oh-sore-us*)

• I am a	bipedal herbivore
• My family was	Ceratopsids
• My name means	'Parrot lizard'
• I lived in the	Early Cretaceous period, about 130 million years ago
• My home was	Asia
• My length was	2.5 metres (8 feet)
• My weight was	50 kilograms (110 pounds)

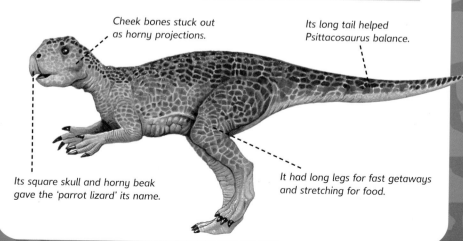

Cheek bones stuck out as horny projections.

Its long tail helped Psittacosaurus balance.

Its square skull and horny beak gave the 'parrot lizard' its name.

It had long legs for fast getaways and stretching for food.

Seismosaurus

(say *size-moh-sore-us*)

• I am a	quadrupedal herbivore
• My family was	Sauropods
• My name means	'Earth-shaking lizard'
• I lived in the	Late Jurassic period, about 150 million years ago
• My home was	North America
• My length was	**40 metres** (131 feet)
• My weight was	**30 tonnes** (approx. 30 tons)

Seismosaurus was a long-necked dinosaur, bigger even than its close relative, Diplodocus.

It had a long, whip-like tail which it might have used to lash out at a predator.

Its nostrils were on top of its head.

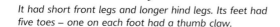

It had short front legs and longer hind legs. Its feet had five toes – one on each foot had a thumb claw.

It had a small head, and peg-like teeth filled the front of its jaws.

Megalosaurus

(say *meg-ah-loh-sore-us*)

• I am a	bipedal carnivore
• My family was	Carnosaurs
• My name means	'Great lizard'
• I lived in the	Middle Jurassic period, about 170 million years ago
• My home was	Europe
• My length was	9 metres (30 feet)
• My weight was	1 tonne (approx. 1 ton)

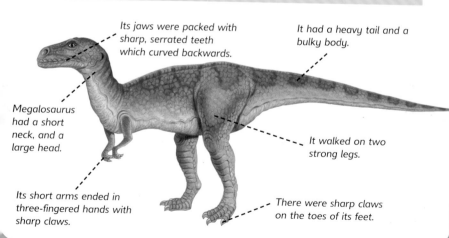

Its jaws were packed with sharp, serrated teeth which curved backwards.

It had a heavy tail and a bulky body.

Megalosaurus had a short neck, and a large head.

Its short arms ended in three-fingered hands with sharp claws.

It walked on two strong legs.

There were sharp claws on the toes of its feet.

Edmontosaurus

(say *ed-mon-toh-sore-us*)

• I am a	bipedal/quadrupedal herbivore
• My family was	Hadrosaurs
• My name means	'Lizard from Edmonton'
• I lived in the	Late Cretaceous period, about 65 million years ago
• My home was	North America
• My length was	13 metres (43 feet)
• My weight was	4 tonnes (approx. 4 tons)

It had large nostrils, covered with folds of skin.

Its head had a broad snout, long jaws with cheek pouches and large eyes. At the tip of its snout was a horny beak-like covering.

Edmontosaurus had a long, pointed tail.

There were as many as 1,000 tiny teeth at the back of its jaws.

It had short arms.

Gallimimus

(say *gal-lee-meem-us*)

• **I am a**	bipedal omnivore
• **My family was**	Ornithomimids
• **My name means**	'Chicken mimic'
• **I lived in the**	Late Cretaceous period, about 70 million years ago
• **My home was**	Asia
• **My length was**	6 metres (20 feet)
• **My weight was**	500 kilograms (1,103 pounds)

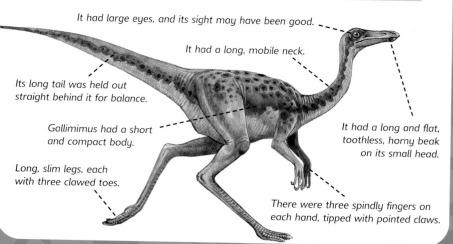

It had large eyes, and its sight may have been good.

It had a long, mobile neck.

Its long tail was held out straight behind it for balance.

Gallimimus had a short and compact body.

Long, slim legs, each with three clawed toes.

It had a long and flat, toothless, horny beak on its small head.

There were three spindly fingers on each hand, tipped with pointed claws.

Protoceratops

(say *pro-toe-ser-a-tops*)

• I am a	quadrupedal herbivore
• My family was	Ceratopsids
• My name means	'First horned face'
• I lived in the	Late Cretaceous period, about 70 million years ago
• My home was	Asia
• My length was	2.7 metres (9 feet)
• My weight was	180 kilograms (400 pounds)

The bony neck frill anchored its jaw muscles and provided some defence against predators.

The bump on its snout may have been used by males in headbutting contests.

It had longer back legs, which were more powerful.

It had shorter front legs with five toes.

It had clawed feet.

The powerful beaked jaws could bite through thick vegetation.

Albertosaurus

(say *al-bur-toh-sore-us*)

• I am a	bipedal carnivore
• My family was	Tyrannosaurs
• My name means	'Lizard from Alberta'
• I lived in the	Late Cretaceous period, about 70 million years ago
• My home was	USA; Canada
• My length was	9 metres (30 feet)
• My weight was	2 tonnes (approx. 2 tons)

Its eyes were on the sides of its head to give good all-round vision.

Its body was balanced by a long, flexible tail.

It had a large head.

Its tiny front arms ended in two small fingers.

It walked on two strong, muscular back legs and was probably a fast runner.

Camarasaurus

(say *kam-are-ah-sore-us*)

• I am a	quadrupedal herbivore
• My family was	Sauropods
• My name means	'Chambered lizard'
• I lived in the	Late Jurassic period, about 150 million years ago
• My home was	North America; Europe
• My length was	18 metres (59 feet)
• My weight was	20 tonnes (approx. 20 tons)

It had a small, long head with a blunt, round snout. Its nostrils were on the top of its head.

Its strong jaws were packed with large spoon-shaped teeth to cut through vegetation.

Its front legs were about the same length as its hind legs, so it stood with its back level to the ground.

Pachycephalosaurus

(say *pack-ee-sef-a-lo-sore-us*)

• I am a	bipedal herbivore
• My family was	Pachycephalosaurs
• My name means	'Thick-headed lizard'
• I lived in the	Late Cretaceous period, about 70 million years ago
• My home was	North America
• My length was	4.6 metres (15 feet)
• My weight was	300 kilograms (660 pounds)

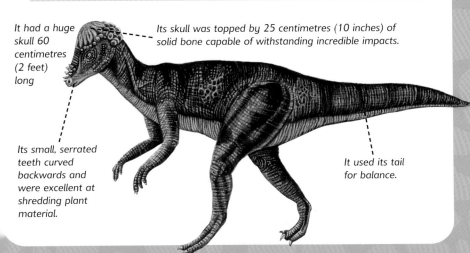

It had a huge skull 60 centimetres (2 feet) long

Its skull was topped by 25 centimetres (10 inches) of solid bone capable of withstanding incredible impacts.

Its small, serrated teeth curved backwards and were excellent at shredding plant material.

It used its tail for balance.

Lycorhinus
(say *lie-koe-rime-us*)

• I am a	bipedal herbivore
• My family was	Heterodontosaurs
• My name means	'Wolf snout'
• I lived in the	Early Jurassic period, about 200 million years ago
• My home was	South Africa
• My length was	1.2 metres (4 feet)
• My weight was	unknown

It had large, slightly curved canine teeth in both its upper and lower jaws.

Strong arms and large, clawed fingers would have been used to catch, or dig for, food.

Wannanosaurus

(say *wan-an-oh-sore-us*)

• I am a	bipedal herbivore
• My family was	Pachycephalosaurs
• My name means	'Wannan lizard'
• I lived in the	Late Cretaceous period, about 85 million years ago
• My home was	Asia
• My length was	60 centimetres (24 inches)
• My weight was	unknown

Wannanosaurus had a small, flat head with a thick, bony skull and tiny brain.

It had a heavy tail held stiffly behind its solidly built body.

It had short arms with clawed fingers.

It had strong hind legs with three-toed clawed feet.

Coelophysis
(say *see-loh-fie-sis*)

• I am a	bipedal carnivore
• My family was	Theropods
• My name means	'Hollow form'
• I lived in the	Late Triassic period, about 220 million years ago
• My home was	North America
• My length was	3 metres (10 feet)
• My weight was	40 kilograms (88 pounds)

It had a long, narrow head, large eyes and a mouth filled with sharp teeth.

Its back legs were very powerful, allowing it to run quickly.

Its leg bones were nearly hollow which kept its weight down – a great help to any animal that relied on speed of attack to chase after and catch its prey.

Its small front legs were used for clawing at food.

Parasaurolophus

(say *pah-rah-sore-oh-loaf-us*)

• I am a	quadrupedal herbivore
• My family was	Hadrosaurs
• My name means	'Beside Saurolophus'
• I lived in the	Late Cretaceous period, about 70 million years ago
• My home was	North America
• My length was	10 metres (33 feet)
• My weight was	3.5 tonnes (approx. 3.5 tons)

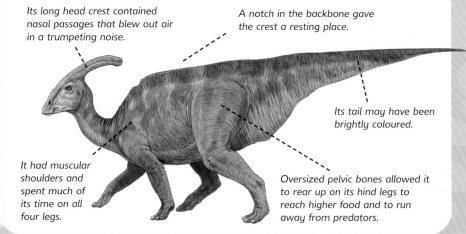

Its long head crest contained nasal passages that blew out air in a trumpeting noise.

A notch in the backbone gave the crest a resting place.

Its tail may have been brightly coloured.

It had muscular shoulders and spent much of its time on all four legs.

Oversized pelvic bones allowed it to rear up on its hind legs to reach higher food and to run away from predators.

Mamenchisaurus

(say *mah-men-chee-sore-us*)

• I am a	quadrupedal herbivore
• My family was	Sauropods
• My name means	'Mamen Brook lizard'
• I lived in the	Late Jurassic period, about 160 million years ago
• My home was	Asia
• My length was	**25 metres** (82 feet)
• My weight was	**27 tonnes** (approx. 27 tons)

It had a very long neck that measured about 14 metres (46 feet). Each of its neck bones was supported by two overlapping rod-like ribs, making its neck quite stiff.

Its skull was box-shaped, and it had strong spoon-shaped teeth.

Mamenchisaurus had a small head.

Its hind legs were longer than its front legs.

Riojasaurus

(say *ree-o-ha-sore-us*)

• I am a	quadrupedal herbivore
• My family was	Prosauropods
• My name means	'Lizard from Rioja'
• I lived in the	Late Triassic period, about 220 million years ago
• My home was	South America
• My length was	10 metres (33 feet)
• My weight was	1 tonne (approx. 1 ton)

It had a long neck and a small head. Inside its mouth were many leaf-shaped, serrated teeth.

Its long, slender tail could be flicked from side to side.

It had a long, heavy body with elephant-like legs and clawed feet. Its leg bones were massive and solidly formed.

Minmi

(say *min-my*)

• I am a	quadrupedal herbivore
• My family was	Ankylosaurs
• My name means	'From Minmi Crossing'
• I lived in the	Early Cretaceous period, about 115 million years ago
• My home was	Australia
• My length was	3 metres (10 feet)
• My weight was	1 tonne (approx. 1 ton)

Its body was covered in bony plates, called scutes.

It had a short neck and turtle-shaped head, a tiny brain and many small, leaf-shaped teeth.

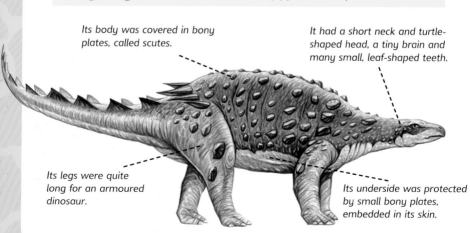

Its legs were quite long for an armoured dinosaur.

Its underside was protected by small bony plates, embedded in its skin.

Plateosaurus

(say *plat-ee-oh-sore-us*)

• I am a	quadrupedal herbivore
• My family was	Prosauropods
• My name means	'Flat reptile'
• I lived in the	Late Triassic period, about 220 million years ago
• My home was	Europe
• My length was	7 metres (23 feet)
• My weight was	2 tonnes (approx. 2 tons)

It had a stronger head than most prosauropods.

Its long neck allowed it to reach food in a wide range of places.

It had small, leaf-shaped teeth for munching plants.

Its long tail allowed Plateosaurus to balance while standing up on hind legs and feeding in upper branches.

Its low-slung lower jaw hinge allowed the jaw muscles greater leverage.

Velociraptor

(say *vel-oh-see-rap-tor*)

• I am a	bipedal carnivore
• My family was	Raptors
• My name means	'Quick plunderer'
• I lived in the	Late Cretaceous period, about 70 million years ago
• My home was	Asia
• My length was	1.8 metres (6 feet)
• My weight was	25 kilograms (55 pounds)

It had a large head and brain cavity. The large brain allowed co-ordinated movement.

Its sharp teeth were for ripping flesh.

Its long tail was used for balance while running and attacking.

Its shorter front legs with three claws were used mainly for gripping prey.

It had longer back legs with powerful muscles for pursuit and attack.

The second toe had a long, sharp, curved claw used for ripping prey.

The third and fourth toes were used to bear weight.

Troodon

(say *troo-oh-don*)

• I am a	bipedal carnivore
• My family was	Raptors
• My name means	'Wounding tooth'
• I lived in the	Late Cretaceous period, about 70 million years ago
• My home was	North America (Alberta)
• My length was	2 metres (7 feet)
• My weight was	40 kilograms (90 pounds)

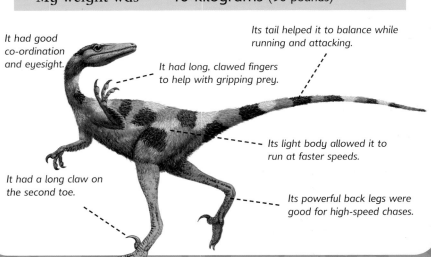

It had good co-ordination and eyesight.

Its tail helped it to balance while running and attacking.

It had long, clawed fingers to help with gripping prey.

Its light body allowed it to run at faster speeds.

It had a long claw on the second toe.

Its powerful back legs were good for high-speed chases.

Corythosaurus

(say *coh-rith-oh-sor-us*)

• I am a	bipedal herbivore
• My family was	Hadrosaurs
• My name means	'Helmet lizard'
• I lived in the	Late Cretaceous period, about 80 million years ago
• My home was	North America
• My length was	10 metres (33 feet)
• My weight was	4 tonnes (approx. 4 tons)

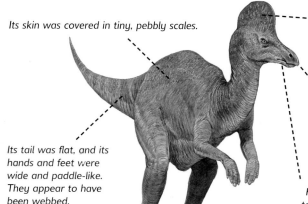

Its skin was covered in tiny, pebbly scales.

It was called 'helmet lizard' because of the distinctive bony crest on top of its head, which resembled a flattened helmet.

Its long, flat beak was used to graze on plants close to the ground.

Its tail was flat, and its hands and feet were wide and paddle-like. They appear to have been webbed.

Hundreds of small, sharp teeth grew inside its jaws.